First Facts®

EASY MAGIC TRICKS

AWESOME
COIN TRICKS

by Steve Charney

CAPSTONE PRESS
a capstone imprint

First Facts is published by Capstone Press,
151 Good Counsel Drive, P.O. Box 669, Mankato, Minnesota 56002.
www.capstonepub.com

 Books published by Capstone Press are manufactured with paper
containing at least 10 percent post-consumer waste.

Library of Congress Cataloging-in-Publication Data
Charney, Steve.
  Awesome coin tricks / by Steve Charney.
    p. cm. — (First facts. Easy magic tricks)
  Includes bibliographical references and index.
  Summary: "Step-by-step instructions and photos describe how to perform
magic coin tricks"—Provided by publisher.
  ISBN 978-1-4296-4514-0 (library binding)
  1. Coin tricks—Juvenile literature. I. Title. II. Series.
  GV1559.C45 2011
  793.8—dc22   2010003662

Editorial Credits
Kathryn Clay, editor; Matt Bruning, designer; Marcy Morin, scheduler;
  Sarah Schuette, photo stylist; Eric Manske, production specialist

Photo Credits
All photos by Capstone Press/Karon Dubke, except Ed Hord, 24

Printed in the United States of America in North Mankato, Minnesota.
072011   006241R

TABLE OF CONTENTS

INTRODUCTION

Did you know piggy banks are full of magic? They really are! All those coins can be used for magic tricks. No piggy bank? No problem. Any coins will work.

Here's a secret **magicians** don't like to tell you. Many tricks take almost no skill! That's the good news. The bad news is you still have to practice to make a trick work. After all, nothing is worse than messing up a trick. Except maybe having your pants fall down on stage! So keep practicing. Once you've mastered the trick, you're ready for an **audience**.

magician—a person who performs magic tricks
audience—people who watch or listen to a play, movie, or show

MAGIC TIP

Magicians never tell how the tricks are done.
Here's why:

1 You can never do the trick again for the same audience.

2 The audience might be disappointed by how simple the trick is.

3 Other magicians could catch you telling their secrets. They might try to saw you in half!

FLIPPED OUT

Have your friend call heads or tails. She will flip when you win every coin toss.

Getting Ready:

Practice feeling the coin in your hand. **Heads** is smoother than **tails**. With practice, you'll be able to feel the difference quickly.

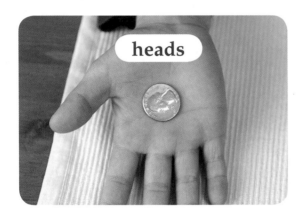

heads

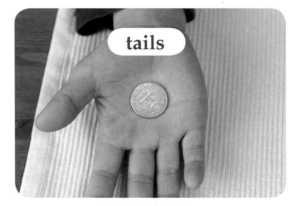

tails

The Trick:

1

Flip a coin. Have your friend call heads or tails while the coin is in the air.

heads—the side of the coin with a person's head
tails—the side of a coin without a person's head

2 Catch the coin in your hand. Quickly make a fist to hide the coin.

3 Feel the coin with your fingers when you catch it. Figure out if the coin is showing heads or tails.

4 The side facing up may be the side your friend called. Then secretly slide your thumb inside your fist and flip the coin over. Show the coin to your friend. You won the coin toss!

MAGIC TIP

It's easiest to feel a coin's different sides with quarters and dimes.

THE COIN DROP

Do you have an **invisible** friend? Well, this is an invisible coin. It disappears in the air and magically shows up in your hand.

The Trick:

1 Hold a coin between the thumb and index finger of your right hand.

2 Reach for the coin with your left hand.

invisible—something you cannot see

3

As you reach for the coin, secretly let it drop into your right hand.

Pull your left hand away. Your friend will think the coin is in your left hand.

4

Throw the invisible coin into the air with your left hand. Pretend to watch it fall. Your friend won't be able to see the coin.

5

Pretend to catch the coin in your right hand.

The coin is no longer invisible. Ta-da!

BOTTLED UP

Show a coin. Show a bottle. Hey! How did that coin get in the bottle? Only you will know.

Getting Ready:

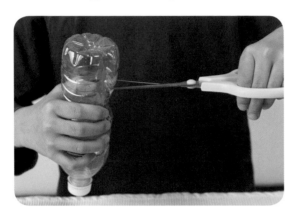

Use a scissors to cut a 1-inch (2.5-centimeter) **slit** near the bottom of a plastic bottle.

The Trick:

1 Tap the bottom and sides of the bottle with a coin. Show the bottle is whole. Your hand should cover the slit.

slit—a narrow cut

2 Unscrew the cap. Show that the bottle is empty.

3 Turn the slit toward you. Tap the coin against the bottle two times. On the third tap, slip it through the slit. Don't let your friend see the slit.

4 Shake the bottle. Turn it upside down. The coin is trapped inside!

MAGIC TIP

No one will see the slit. That means you too. So remember where it is. When you're ready to push in the coin, press down on the slit. This will help the coin slide in smoothly and quietly.

JOE'S MOM

Here's a riddle you can repeat over and over. People rarely get the right answer. But they sure come up with funny wrong answers.

• • • • • **Getting Ready:**

Place a nickel, a dime, and a penny on a table.

• • • • • **The Trick:**

Point to the penny. Say, "Joe's mom has three kids. The first kid is named Penny."

2

Point to the nickel.
Say, "The second kid
is named Nickel."

3

Pick up the dime.
Say, "And the third
kid is named … ?"

4

Wait for your friend
to say "Dime."
Few people get
the right answer.

5

Tell your friend that
the answer is … Joe!
If Joe's mom had
three kids, one of
them has to be Joe!

ELBOW COIN SNATCH

So you think you're fast? Great! This trick needs some speed. Drop a coin from your elbow. Then quickly catch it in your hand.

• • • • • • • The Trick:

1

Bend your arm so your hand is next to your ear. Your elbow should point up.

This trick can be difficult to master. If you don't catch the coin the first time, just keep trying until you catch it.

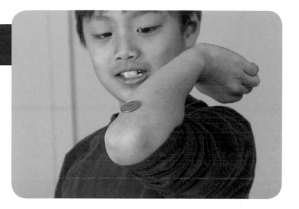

Balance a coin on your elbow.

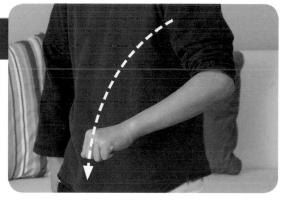

Drop your elbow quickly. Your hand will come forward. Grab the coin with your hand as it falls.

Show your friend you caught the coin. She will be amazed by your speedy skills!

FUNNY BONE MAGIC

What's so funny about your funny bone? It has magical powers that make coins disappear.

The Trick:

1 Bend your right arm. Your hand is near your ear. Your elbow faces up.

2 Pick up a coin with your left hand. Rub it on your elbow. Say, "This coin will disappear into my funny bone."

3 Let go of the coin. The coin will fall.

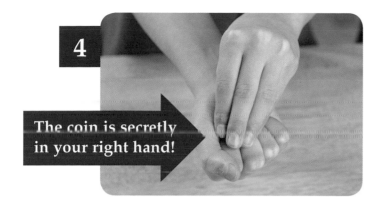

4

The coin is secretly in your right hand!

Say, "I'll try again." Pick up the coin with your right hand. Grab for it with your left hand but don't actually take the coin. Your friend will think the coin is in your left hand.

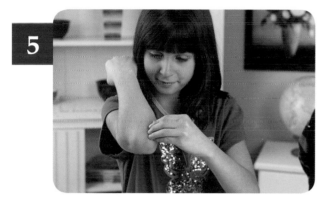

5

Rub your elbow with your left hand. Your right hand drops the coin down your shirt.

6

Take your left hand away. The coin has disappeared!

MAGIC TIP

You can keep the coin in your right hand. Then make it appear from your ear or armpit.

MAKING CHANGE

Why are so many magicians broke? They keep turning quarters into nickels! Now you can too. Here's how.

• • • • • • **The Trick:**

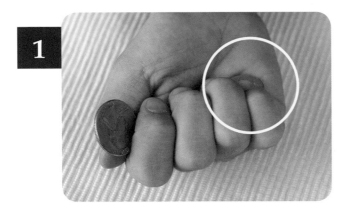

1 Hold a quarter between your right thumb and index finger. Hide a nickel in your palm under your three other fingers.

2 Pretend to throw the quarter into the air. Throw just the nickel instead.

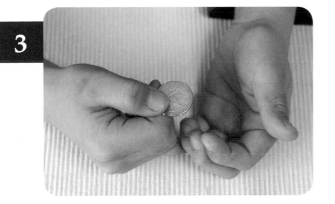

3

While your friend is watching the nickel in the air, secretly put the quarter in your left hand.

4

Catch the nickel and show it. The quarter has turned into a nickel!

MAGIC TIP

Look up as you throw the coin. That way your friend will look too. She won't see you put the quarter into your left hand.

DISAPPEARING CRAYON

Your friend will be looking at the coin. But the real trick is making the crayon disappear.

Getting Ready:

Hold a coin in one hand and a crayon in the other.

The Trick:

1

Say, "This coin will disappear with the help of my magic crayon." Lift the crayon to your ear. Quickly swing it down toward the coin.

2

When the crayon touches the coin, say a silly magic word like "Shazooley!" Nothing happens.

Try again. Lift the crayon to your ear and swing it down. Still nothing happens. Say, "Give me one more chance."

Lift the crayon a third time. When the crayon is near your head, secretly tuck it behind your ear.

Swing your hand down. The crayon is gone! Act surprised and say, "I guess my magic crayon disappeared."

After a while, turn your head. Your friend will laugh when he sees the crayon behind your ear.

MAGIC TIP

Using the coin is called misdirection. As you do the trick, hold the coin close to your friend. Move the coin around. Your friend will be looking at the coin, not the crayon.

misdirection—to draw attention to a spot where the trick is not taking place

GLOSSARY

audience (AW-dee-uhns)—people who watch or listen to a play, movie, or show

heads (HEDS)—the side of the coin with a person's head

invisible (in-VIZ-uh-buhl)—something you cannot see

magician (ma-JI-shuhn)—a person who performs magic tricks

misdirection (mis-di-REK-shuhn)—to draw attention to a spot where the trick is not taking place

slit (SLIT)—a narrow cut

tails (TAYLS)—the side of a coin without a person's head

READ MORE

Barnhart, Norm. *Amazing Magic Tricks: Beginner Level*. Magic Tricks. Mankato, Minn.: Capstone Press, 2009.

Charney, Steve. *Hocus-Jokus: How to Do Funny Magic*. Minnetonka, Minn.: Meadowbrook Press, 2003.

Fullman, Joe. *Coin and Rope Tricks*. Magic Handbook. Laguna Hills, Calif: QEB Pub., 2008.

INTERNET SITES

FactHound offers a safe, fun way to find Internet sites related to this book. All of the sites on FactHound have been researched by our staff.

Here's all you do:

Visit *www.facthound.com*

Type in this code: 9781429645140

INDEX

ABOUT THE AUTHOR

Steve Charney learned magic when he was a little kid. Now he performs more than 100 times each year.

Steve is also a ventriloquist, radio personality, musician, and songwriter. He has written songbooks, storybooks, joke books, and magic books. Look for his performances on the Internet.